Planting and Growing

Gail Blasser Riley

Photographs by Ken O'Donoghue

Rigby

A Harcourt Achieve Imprint

www.Rigby.com
1-800-531-5015

I'm going to grow peppers.

I need seeds.

What else do I need?

I'm going to grow peppers.
I need seeds and soil.
What else do I need?

I'm going to grow peppers.
I need seeds, soil, and
a pot.
How can I help
my pepper seeds grow?

First I put soil into the pot.

Then I dig a hole
with my finger.
I put the seeds in the hole.

Next I put soil on the seeds.
I water them.

Last I put the seeds
in the sun.
The soil, water, and
sun will help the seeds
grow into peppers.

Things I Need
for Planting and Growing

 seeds

 water

 soil

sun

 pot